WATER RESCUE DOGS

by Frances E. Ruffin

Consultant: Wilma Melville, Founder
National Disaster Search Dog Foundation

PUBLISHING COMPANY, INC.

New York, New York

Special thanks to Wilma Melville who founded the:
National Disaster Search Dog Foundation
206 N. Signal Street, Suite R
Ojai, CA 93023
(888) 4K9-HERO
www.SearchDogFoundation.org

The Search Dog Foundation is a not-for-profit organization that rescues dogs, gives them professional training, and partners them with firefighters to find people buried alive in disasters. They produce the most highly trained search dogs in the nation.

To Billy Atkins, who was a great dog lover

Original design and production by Dawn Beard Creative and Octavo Design and Production, Inc.

Credits

Cover, Front (left), Werner Layer / Animals Animals; (all others), AP / Wide World Photos; Back (all), AP / Wide World Photos. Title page, Werner Layer / Animals Animals. Page 3, AP / Wide World Photos; 4–5, Alamy Images; 5, Chet Jezierski; 6–7 (both), courtesy, Betsy Wiederhold, Seawied Newfoundlands; 8–9, Forestier Yves / Corbis Sygma; 9, Cheryl A. Ertelt / Photos & Phrases; 10–11, Tom Nebbia / Corbis; 11, FLPA / Alamy; 12–13, Parks Canada # 81-2-930-010 from Gros Morne National Park Historic Photo Collection; 13, AP / Wide World Photos; 14, Forestier Yves / Corbis Sygma; 14–15, Tyrrell Mendis, The Impressionists; 16–17, AP / Wide World Photos; 17, Lt. Col. Mark J. Reardon, U.S. Army Center of Military History's Lewis and Clark Commemorative Office, Corps of Discovery; 18–19, Betty McDonnell / Kilyka Newfoundlands; 20–21, Howard M Paul / Emergency Stock; 21, AP / Wide World Photos; 22–23, Forestier Yves / Corbis Sygma; 23, 24–25, AP / Wide World Photos; 25, 911 Pictures; 26, Chet Jezierski; 26–27, Reynolds Stock Photo; 28, Scott Warren / Aurora Photos; 29(top left), John Daniels / Ardea.com; 29(top right), PhotoSpin.com; 29(bottom left), Alamy Images; 29(bottom right), Fotosearch.com.

Library of Congress Cataloging-in-Publication Data

Ruffin, Frances E.
Water rescue dogs / by Frances E. Ruffin.
 p. cm.— (Dog heroes)
Includes bibliographical references (p.   ) and index.
ISBN 1-59716-142-X (lib. bdg.)—ISBN 1-59716-144-6 (pbk.)
1. Water rescue dogs—Juvenile literature. I. Title. II. Series.

SF429.55.R84 2006
636.7'088'6—dc22

2005008961

For more information, write to Bearport Publishing Company, Inc., 101 Fifth Avenue, Suite 6R, New York, New York 10003. Printed in the United States of America.

1 2 3 4 5 6 7 8 9 10

Table of Contents

Lost in a Storm   4

Ursa to the Rescue   6

WET DOG   8

WETT   10

Stranded!   12

Tang Gets a Medal   14

Sea Dogs   16

Water-Loving Puppies   18

Air Scenting   20

Born to Save   22

More "Search"
    Than "Rescue"   24

Great Water Rescue Dogs   26

Just the Facts   28

Common Breeds:
    Water Rescue Dogs   29

Glossary   30

Bibliography   31

Read More   31

Learn More Online   31

Index   32

About the Author   32

Lost in a Storm

Lightning flashed across the dark night sky as the wind began to blow. Meanwhile, Elizabeth's motorboat chugged across the choppy waters of Maine's Penobscot Bay. Elizabeth had to get to her island home before the storm got worse.

Penobscot Bay

She knew she must be close. The fog was so thick, however, that she couldn't see the island's shore.

Then **disaster** struck. The boat's motor died, and water began to flood the **deck**. Crying, Elizabeth yelled into the darkness for help.

Through the roar of the wind, she began to hear a high, squeaky bark. It was Ursa, her Newfoundland.

A Newfoundland

A Newfoundland, or a Newfie, is a type of large dog with a heavy, waterproof coat of fur. These dogs love to swim.

Ursa to the Rescue

The dog must have heard Elizabeth's cry for help. Ursa quickly jumped off the rocks at the shore and began swimming toward the boat!

Elizabeth's flashlight beam soon found Ursa in the water. She took hold of the dog so the animal could rest from her swim. Ursa playfully tried to snatch Elizabeth's hat, which gave her an idea. She tied a rope around the hat and put it in Ursa's mouth.

Elizabeth and her Newfie, Paw

"You're going to show me the way home," Elizabeth yelled. She threw the rope into the water. Ursa grabbed it and began to swim toward shore. Elizabeth tried the motor again and got it started.

At one time, fishermen used Newfies to help pull nets out of the water.

Ursa

WET DOG

Elizabeth kept the flashlight on Ursa as the dog guided the boat back to the island. Ursa had saved Elizabeth's life!

A fit Newfie can easily tow a rubber life raft for two miles (3 km) in water. A large raft may carry as many as 20 people.

Today, many groups train dogs for water rescues. One is called WET DOG, which stands for _Water _Education and _Training _Dog **Obedience** _Group. WET DOG trains animals to pass a special test.

The test has several parts. The dog has to **retrieve** an object thrown into the water. He has to tow a boat 50 feet (15 m) in deep water. Then he has to carry a **lifeline** out to a swimmer.

Like the dog above, WET DOG has each animal retrieve a life vest as part of its water rescue test. The vest is thrown from a boat when the dog isn't looking.

WETT

WET DOG also makes the dog and **handler** swim far from shore. Then the dog tows the handler back to land.

The last part of the test is the hardest. The dog swims out alone to rescue a person who's pretending to be in trouble.

Newfoundlands practice water rescue

If the dog passes all parts of the test, he or she is given a WET DOG title called WETT. The letters stand for Water Education and Training Tested. The dog's owner can then use the letters WETT after the dog's name.

Any breed of dog, large or small, can make a water rescue. Amazingly, even a ten-pound (5-kg) Chihuahua has passed the WET DOG test!

Stranded!

One of the most famous sea rescues in North America was made by a dog. In 1919, a storm raged off the coast of Newfoundland, a Canadian island. *Ethie*, a steamship, crashed onto rocks just off shore. The **stranded** ship was filled with crew and passengers. The captain needed a way to reach rescuers waiting on land.

The *Ethie* at its final resting place

According to **legend**, the captain's huge black dog, Tang, was also on board. The captain placed one end of a rope in Tang's mouth. Holding the rope between his teeth, Tang leaped into the ocean and swam to shore.

A pit bull named Weela led her owner through a flooded farm to bring food to the animals. The food saved the lives of 29 dogs, 13 horses, and one cat.

A pit bull

Tang Gets a Medal

Reaching the rescuers was not easy. Tang was tossed around by the icy waves. The wind blew salt water into his eyes. Many times, he was almost dragged out to sea by the storm. The brave dog, however, swam on until he reached the rescue party. There, one of the men on shore grabbed the rope Tang carried. He fastened it to a post.

Aboard ships, Newfoundlands were known for their sensitive noses. The dogs could smell land well before sailors could see the shore.

The rescuers were able to pull the boat to safety. Tang saved more than 90 lives. In honor of his bravery, the dog was given a medal. People say he wore it every day for the rest of his life.

Visitors to Newfoundland can still see the remains of the *Ethie*.

Sea Dogs

Tang and Ursa were both Newfoundlands. This breed is famous for rescuing people at sea. In fact, Newfoundlands are nicknamed the "lifeguard dog." They even patrol beaches in Britain, France, and Italy.

Newfies are large, bearlike animals. Fully grown, they can weigh more than 150 pounds (68 kg). These water-loving giants were commonly found on ships during the 18th and 19th centuries.

Golden retrievers and Labrador retrievers also make good water rescue dogs. They are strong swimmers, large and big enough to handle heavy objects in water. They also have an **instinct** for retrieving.

In 1803, a Newfoundland named Seaman was a member of the Lewis and Clark expedition. He crossed America with these explorers. This statue in St. Charles, Missouri, honors the explorers.

Water-Loving Puppies

From a young age, some puppies are trained to be water rescue dogs. When just four months old, these pups begin to play in a swimming pool. Their trainers get in the pool with them. This play helps them learn to be **confident** in the water.

Water search and rescue pups learn to work in forests, mountains, and at seashores. They are trained to be calm in vehicles, such as boats and helicopters.

The puppies also practice retrieving objects in water. Some trainers attach a weight to a dog's favorite toy. Then they let the toy sink at the shallow end of the pool. The dog is taught to **fetch** it. As the puppy learns this skill, the toy is dropped into deeper and deeper water.

Air Scenting

Drowning **victims** are often **submerged** under many feet of water. Rescuers find these people by using air-scenting dogs. These animals locate bodies as far down as 35 feet (11 m). Rescuers can then dive in and bring the victims to the surface.

How do the dogs locate the bodies? Each person has a **scent** that floats in the air. The scent of a person underwater comes up to the water's surface in air bubbles. It's then carried along by the wind. Air-scenting dogs follow the scent to the place where the bubbles first broke the surface.

Tracer, a Portuguese Water Dog, has just picked up the scent of a diver in ten feet (3 m) of water.

Air-scenting dogs can detect bodies up to 48 hours after they have been submerged.

Born to Save

When a water rescue dog spots someone in trouble, he first swims out to the person. Then he circles the victim. Once the person gets a hold of the dog's shoulder, the dog heads back to shore.

During an accident in water, however, a person may be **unconscious** and unable to move. A rescue dog still knows what to do. He first grabs the victim's arm in his teeth. Then he rolls the person on her back to keep her face out of the water. Finally, the dog drags the person back to the shore and then runs for help.

Water rescue dogs are taught not to be afraid of people who are wearing diving gear. Here, Robin Hood gives a big kiss to diver Barry Kromer.

Water rescue dogs are trained to know when a person in the water needs help or is just playing.

More "Search" Than "Rescue"

Today, many communities use specially trained dogs to look for drowning victims. Often, the animals work from the shore. When they smell a human scent, they swim out to the spot it is coming from. This action shows their handlers exactly where to send divers to recover a body.

Sometimes, the dogs work from police boats. Most water rescue animals are part of a city or state police department. After floods and boating accidents, police emergency workers take the dogs to search for **survivors**. Sadly, however, most of the people that they or their dogs find have drowned.

In the United States, about 100 people lose their lives in boating accidents or floods every year.

Great Water Rescue Dogs

Animals that work in water rescue must be in good physical shape. Swimming is hard work. Towing people in water is even harder work. For these reasons, younger animals make the best rescuers.

In 1995, two black Labrador retrievers made the *Guinness Book of World Records*. The dogs and their owner swam 9.5 miles (15.2 km) in six hours in the Maui, Hawaii Channel.

After about seven years on the job, most water rescue dogs retire. They've become heroes to many of the people they've met. They've often saved lives, found missing people, and been great companions to the humans they've worked with. They deserve to spend the rest of their lives as honored members of their human families.

Just the Facts

- Newfies are natural water dogs. Their feet are webbed, like a duck. They have a long tail that they can use like a boat's rudder to guide them.

- Newfies do not "dog paddle." They swim by sweeping their legs to the side. Their webbed paws are spread wide to get the greatest pull in the water.

- Newfies are able to pull more than 2,000 pounds (907 kg).

- Nana, the dog in the book *Peter Pan*, is a Newfoundland.

- On most airlines, search dogs can travel with people. Their handlers, however, must travel with them.

- Portuguese water dogs are another popular breed of water rescue dogs. Like Newfies, they have webbed feet and love the water.

- There are about 100 water search teams in the United States.

A water rescue dog being trained to search for bodies

Common Breeds: WATER RESCUE DOGS

Portuguese Water Dog

golden retriever

Newfoundland

Labrador retriever

Glossary

breed (BREED) type of a certain animal

confident (KON-fuh-duhnt) belief in one's abilities

deck (DEK) the floor of a ship or boat

disaster (duh-ZASS-tur) a sudden event causing much damage, loss, or suffering

fetch (FECH) to go after something and then bring it back

handler (HAND-lur) someone who trains and works with animals

instinct (IN-stingkt) a natural ability

legend (LEJ-und) a story that has been passed down from years ago

lifeline (LIFE-line) a piece of rope that is used to save someone's life

obedience (oh-BEE-dee-uns) the act of following good behavior and rules

retrieve (ri-TREEV) bring something back

scent (SENT) the smell of an animal or person

stranded (STRAND-ed) left in a lonely or dangerous position

submerged (suhb-MURJED) underwater or below the surface of another liquid

survivors (sur-VYE-vurs) people who live through a disaster

tow (TOH) to pull something

unconscious (uhn-KON-shuhss) not awake

victims (VIK-tuhmz) people who have been hurt or killed

Bibliography

Budiansky, Stephen. *The Truth About Dogs: An Inquiry into the Ancestry, Social Conventions, Mental Habits, and Moral Fiber of* Canis familiaris. New York: Viking (2000).

Jones, Tim. *Dog Heroes: True Stories About Extraordinary Animals Around the World.* Seattle, WA: Epicenter Press (1995).

Owens, Carrie. *Working Dogs.* Rocklin, CA: Prima Publishing (1999).

Steiger, Brad, and Sherry Hansen Steiger. *Dog Miracles: Inspirational and Heroic True Stories.* Avon, MA: Adams Media Corporation (2001).

Weisbord, Merrily, and Kim Kachanoff. *Dogs with Jobs: Working Dogs Around the World.* New York: Atria (2000).

Read More

Aller, Susan Bivin. *Emma and the Night Dogs.* Morton Grove, IL: Albert Whitman & Co. (1997).

American Kennel Club. *The Complete Dog Book for Kids.* New York: Hungry Minds, Inc. (1996).

Bulanda, Susan. *Ready! The Training of the Search and Rescue Dog.* Irvine, CA: Doral Publishing (1994).

Harlow, Joan Hiatt. *Star in the Storm.* New York: Simon & Schuster (2000).

Learn More Online

Visit these Web sites to learn more about water rescue dogs:

www.akc.org

www.cncnewfs.com/

www.osanewf.com

www.wetdog.org/faq.htm

Index

air scenting 20–21

boating accidents 25
breeds 11, 16, 28, 29

Chihuahua 11

drowning 20, 24–25

Ethie 12, 15

floods 13, 25

golden retrievers 17, 29
*Guinness Book of World
    Records* 26

handler 10, 24, 28

Labrador retrievers 17,
    26, 29
Lewis and Clark 17
life vest 9

Maine 4

Newfoundlands (Newfies)
    5, 6–7, 8, 10, 14, 16–17,
    28–29
North America 12

obedience 9

Penobscot Bay 4
Peter Pan 28
Portuguese Water Dog
    21, 28, 29
puppies 18–19

retrieve 9, 17, 19

scent 21, 24
Seaman 17
storm 4–5, 12, 14
submerged 20–21
swimming 5, 6–7, 10, 13,
    14, 17, 18, 22, 24, 26, 28

Tang 13, 14–15, 16
tests 9, 10–11
towing 8–9, 10, 26
training 9, 11, 18–19, 23, 24

Ursa 5, 6–7, 8, 16

Weela 13
WET DOG 8–9, 10–11
WETT 10–11

About the Author

Frances E. Ruffin writes nonfiction books for children.
She is a dog lover who lives in New York, a city of dog lovers.
This is her second book about dogs.